TRENDLINE TRADING

STRATEGIES:

A COMPREHENSIVE GUIDE TO MASTERING FOREX TRADING WITH TRENDLINES

BY SIBUSISO NSIBANDE

To the ones who work hard every day to make ends meet, those who hustle and grind through the struggle, never accepting defeat, those who strive to better themselves and their loved ones,

This book is for you, the unsung heroes who keep pushing until the job is done.

May the knowledge within these pages help you on your journey to success. And may your efforts be rewarded with prosperity, happiness, and progress.

Remember that every step counts, and every effort is worth it in the end,

So keep pushing forward, my friends, and never give up on your dreams again.

Contents

Introduction

Forex trading can be a challenging and intimidating endeavor, especially for those who are just starting out. It can be difficult to know where to begin, which strategies to use, and how to minimize your risk while maximizing your profits. That's where this book comes in.

"Trendline Trading Strategies: A Comprehensive Guide to Mastering Forex Trading with Trendlines" is designed to provide you with a complete understanding of trendline trading strategies in Forex. By the time you finish reading this book, you will have gained a deep understanding of how to use trendlines to your advantage when trading Forex.

The book is written in a clear and concise manner, making it easy to understand for both beginner and advanced traders. Each chapter covers a different aspect of trendline trading, including identifying trendlines, trading breakouts, using trendlines for entry and exit points, risk management, backtesting, and more.

The first few chapters of the book are dedicated to providing you with a solid foundation in understanding what trendlines are and how to identify them in the Forex market. From there, the book takes a deep dive into specific strategies for using trendlines to trade the Forex market. You'll learn how to trade an uptrend, a downtrend, a horizontal trend, and even a trendline channel.

In addition to providing detailed explanations of trendline trading strategies, this book also includes practical tips, real-world examples, and case studies to help you apply what you've learned. You'll also learn how to backtest and optimize your strategies, as well as manage your emotions and monitor your trades for optimal results.

Finally, this book is dedicated to helping you achieve your financial goals. The last few chapters are dedicated to risk management, emotional control, and withdrawing profits. You'll learn how to minimize your losses, maintain discipline, and when to withdraw your profits to maximize your returns.

Whether you're a beginner or an experienced trader, "Trendline Trading Strategies" is an essential resource for anyone looking to master Forex trading with trendlines. So, grab your copy today and start your journey towards becoming a successful Forex trader!

Chapter 1:

Explanation of Trendlines and their Importance in Forex Trading

In forex trading, a trendline is a straight line that connects two or more price points on a chart. These price points are usually the highs or lows of a given asset's price movement. Trendlines are used to identify the direction of a trend and can be either uptrends or downtrends. They are important in forex trading because they help traders to identify potential entry and exit points, as well as support and resistance levels.

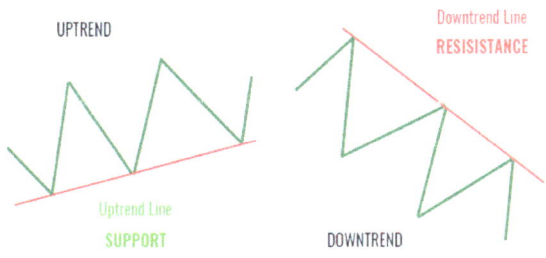

A trendline that connects two or more higher lows is known as an uptrend line. An uptrend line is a visual representation of a bullish market where the price of the asset is increasing. In contrast, a trendline that connects two or more lower highs is known as a downtrend line. A downtrend line is a visual representation of a bearish market where the price of the asset is decreasing.

The importance of trendlines in forex trading cannot be overstated. Trendlines are a simple yet effective way of understanding the direction of the market, and they help traders to identify potential buying or selling opportunities. When a market is trending upwards, traders may look for opportunities to buy the asset at a price point where the trendline meets the current price. Similarly, when a market is trending downwards, traders may look for opportunities to sell the asset at a price point where the trendline meets the current price.

Trendlines also help traders to identify key support and resistance levels. A support level is a price point at which the asset's price is expected to stop declining and start rising again. A resistance level is a price point at which the asset's price is expected to stop rising and start declining again. These levels are important because they can help traders to identify potential entry and exit points.

In conclusion, trendlines are an important tool in forex trading because they help traders to identify the direction of the market, potential entry and exit points, and support and resistance levels. By understanding how to draw and use trendlines, traders can make more informed trading decisions and improve their overall performance in the forex market.

Chapter 2:

Identifying Trendlines

Identifying trendlines is a crucial step in a trendline strategy. Trendlines are used to identify the direction of a trend and potential areas of support and resistance. In this chapter, we will discuss how to identify trendlines and different types of trendlines.

I. Identifying Trendlines

To identify a trendline, a trader should look for two or more points on a chart that show a trend in either an upward or downward direction. For an upward trendline, traders should look for two or more price points with higher lows. For a downward trendline, traders should look for two or more price points with lower highs.

Trendlines should be drawn as straight lines that connect the identified points. Once a trendline is drawn, traders can use it to identify potential areas of support and resistance. Support levels are areas where the price of an asset is likely to bounce back after a decline, while resistance levels are areas where the price is likely to face selling pressure after an advance.

II. Types of Trendlines

There are three main types of trendlines: uptrend, downtrend, and horizontal trendlines.

A. Uptrend Trendlines:

An uptrend trendline is drawn by connecting two or more price points with higher lows. Uptrend trendlines indicate that buyers are in control of the market, and the price of an asset is likely to continue rising until the trendline is broken.

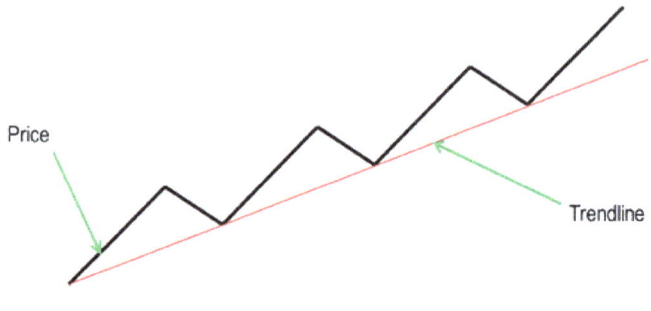

Figure 2: Uptrend

How to trade and uptrend?

Trading an uptrend involves buying an asset as the price rises and holding it until the trend starts to reverse. The following are the steps to trade an uptrend:

1. Identify the Uptrend:

The first step is to identify an uptrend using a trendline or other technical indicators such as moving averages or the Relative Strength Index (RSI). An uptrend is characterized by higher highs and higher lows.

2. Look for Buying Opportunities:

Once an uptrend is identified, traders should look for buying opportunities. This can include buying on pullbacks to the trendline or other support levels, or buying when the price breaks above a resistance level.

3. Set Stop-Loss Orders:

To manage risk, traders should set stop-loss orders below the trendline or support level. This helps to limit potential losses if the trend reverses.

4. Take Profits:

Traders should take profits as the price rises, either by setting a profit target or trailing stop-loss orders. It is important to not be too greedy and to take profits when the trend starts to show signs of exhaustion.

5. Monitor the Trend:

Traders should monitor the uptrend regularly and adjust their trading strategy if the trend starts to show signs of weakening or reversing. This includes identifying potential areas of resistance and support levels that may impact the trend.

6. Practice Proper Risk Management:

Risk management is an essential aspect of trading an uptrend. Traders should not risk more than they can afford to lose, and should use appropriate position sizing and leverage to manage their risk.

In summary, trading an uptrend involves identifying the trend, looking for buying opportunities, setting stop-loss orders, taking profits, monitoring the trend, and practicing proper risk management. By following these steps, traders can maximize their profits and minimize their losses when trading an uptrend in financial markets.

B. Downtrend Trendlines:

A downtrend trendline is drawn by connecting two or more price points with lower highs. Downtrend trendlines indicate that sellers are in control of the market, and the price of an asset is likely to continue falling until the trendline is broken.

Figure 3 Downtrend

How to trade a down trend?

Trading a downtrend involves selling an asset as the price falls and holding it until the trend starts to reverse. The following are the steps to trade a downtrend:

1) Identify the Downtrend:

The first step is to identify a downtrend using a trendline or other technical indicators such as moving averages or the Relative Strength Index (RSI). A downtrend is characterized by lower lows and lower highs.

2) Look for Selling Opportunities:

Once a downtrend is identified, traders should look for selling opportunities. This can include selling on rallies to the trendline or other resistance levels, or selling when the price breaks below a support level.

3) Set Stop-Loss Orders:

To manage risk, traders should set stop-loss orders above the trendline or resistance level.

This helps to limit potential losses if the trend reverses.

4) Take Profits:

Traders should take profits as the price falls, either by setting a profit target or trailing stop-loss orders. It is important to not be too greedy and to take profits when the trend starts to show signs of exhaustion.

5) Monitor the Trend:

Traders should monitor the downtrend regularly and adjust their trading strategy if the trend starts to show signs of weakening or reversing. This includes identifying potential areas of support and resistance levels that may impact the trend.

6) Practice Proper Risk Management:

Risk management is an essential aspect of trading a downtrend. Traders should not risk more than they can afford to lose, and should use appropriate position sizing and leverage to manage their risk.

In summary, trading a downtrend involves identifying the trend, looking for selling opportunities, setting stop-loss orders, taking profits, monitoring the trend, and practicing proper risk management. By following these steps, traders can maximize their profits and minimize their losses when trading a downtrend in financial markets.

C. Horizontal Trendlines:

Horizontal trendlines are drawn by connecting two or more price points at the same price level. These trendlines indicate areas of support and resistance where the price of an asset is likely to stall or reverse.

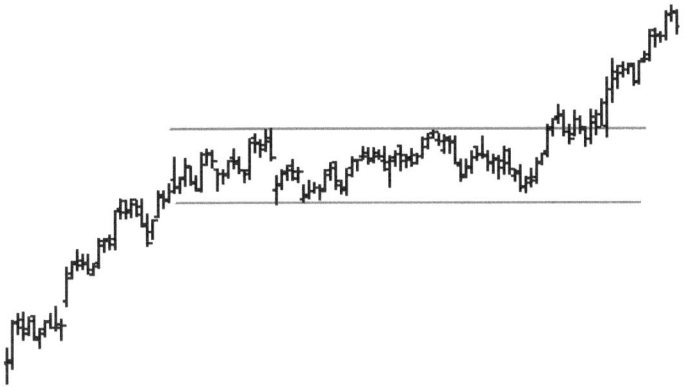

Figure 4 Horizontal Trendlines

In conclusion, identifying trendlines is a crucial step in a trendline strategy. Traders should look for two or more price points that show a trend in either an upward or downward direction or draw straight lines that connect them. Different types of trendlines, including uptrend, downtrend, and horizontal trendlines, can help traders to identify potential areas of support and resistance in financial markets.

How to trade horizontal Trendlines?

Trading horizontal trendlines involves identifying key support and resistance levels that have held up in the past and may do so again in the future. The following are the steps to trade horizontal trendlines:

1. Identify Key Support and Resistance Levels:

The first step is to identify key support and resistance levels on the chart. These levels can be identified using horizontal trendlines or other technical indicators such as pivot points.

2. Look for Trading Opportunities:

Once key support and resistance levels have been identified, traders should look for trading opportunities. This can include buying near support levels and selling near resistance levels.

3. Set Stop-Loss Orders:

To manage risk, traders should set stop-loss orders below support levels when buying and above resistance levels when selling. This helps to limit potential losses if the price breaks below support or above resistance.

4. Take Profits:

Traders should take profits when the price reaches the opposite side of the trading range, either by setting a profit target or trailing stop-loss orders. It is important to not be too greedy and to take profits when the price starts to show signs of reversing.

5. Monitor the Trend:

Traders should monitor the price action around key support and resistance levels regularly and adjust their trading strategy if the price starts to show signs of breaking out or reversing.

6. Practice Proper Risk Management:

Risk management is an essential aspect of trading horizontal trendlines. Traders should not risk more than they can afford to lose, and should use appropriate position sizing and leverage to manage their risk.

In summary, trading horizontal trendlines involves identifying key support and resistance levels, looking for trading opportunities, setting stop-loss orders, taking profits, monitoring the trend, and practicing proper risk management. By following these steps, traders can maximize their profits and minimize their losses when trading horizontal trendlines in financial markets.

Chapter 3:

Support and Resistance

Support and resistance are key concepts in technical analysis that help traders identify levels where the price may stall or reverse. Support refers to a level where buying pressure is strong enough to prevent the price from falling further, while resistance refers to a level where selling pressure is strong enough to prevent the price from rising further.

Identifying Support and Resistance Levels:

Traders can identify support and resistance levels by looking for areas on the chart where the price has bounced off or reversed multiple times. These levels can be identified using trendlines, moving averages, or other technical indicators.

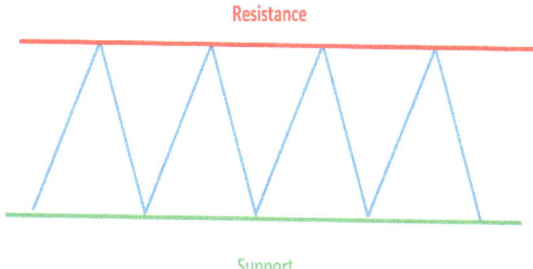

Figure 5 Support and Resistance

Trading Support and Resistance:

Traders can trade support and resistance levels by buying at support and selling at resistance. This can involve entering a trade when the price bounces off a support level or when it breaks above a resistance level.

1. Stop-Loss Orders:

To manage risk, traders should set stop-loss orders below support levels when buying and above resistance levels when selling. This helps

19

to limit potential losses if the price breaks below support or above resistance.

2. Take-Profit Orders:

Traders should take profits when the price reaches the opposite side of the trading range, either by setting a profit target or trailing stop-loss orders. It is important to not be too greedy and to take profits when the price starts to show signs of reversing.

3. Trading Breakouts:

When the price breaks above or below a support or resistance level, this can indicate a potential trend reversal. Traders can enter a trade in the direction of the breakout and set stop-loss orders on the opposite side of the breakout level.

4. Confirming Support and Resistance:

Traders should also look for confirmation of support and resistance levels using other technical indicators such as volume or momentum oscillators. This can help to validate the strength of the support or resistance level and increase the likelihood of a successful trade.

In summary, support and resistance are key concepts in technical analysis that can help traders identify potential trading opportunities and manage their risk. By identifying key support and resistance levels, setting stop-loss and take-profit orders, and confirming support and resistance with other technical indicators, traders can maximize their profits and minimize their losses when trading support and resistance levels in financial markets.

Chapter 4:

Trading Breakouts

Trading breakouts is a popular strategy used by traders to capitalize on significant price movements when the price breaks out of a key level of support or resistance. Here are the steps involved in trading breakouts:

Figure 6 Breakout

1. Identifying Key Levels of Support or Resistance:

The first step in trading breakouts is to identify key levels of support or resistance on the chart. These levels can be identified using trendlines, moving averages, or other technical indicators.

2. Confirming the Breakout:

Once a potential breakout level has been identified, traders should wait for confirmation that the breakout has occurred. This can involve waiting for the price to close above or below the key level of support or resistance, or waiting for a significant price movement in the direction of the breakout.

3. Entering the Trade:

When the breakout is confirmed, traders can enter the trade in the direction of the breakout. This can involve buying when the price breaks above resistance or selling when the price breaks below support.

4. Setting Stop-Loss Orders:

To manage risk, traders should set stop-loss orders below the breakout level when buying and above the breakout level when selling. This helps to limit potential losses if the price breaks back below support or above resistance.

5. Taking Profit:

Traders should take profits when the price reaches the target level or shows signs of reversing. This can involve setting a profit target or using a trailing stop-loss order to lock in profits as the price moves in the direction of the breakout.

6. Monitoring the Trade:

Traders should monitor the trade regularly to ensure that the price continues to move in the direction of the breakout. If the price shows signs of reversing or failing to reach the target level, traders may consider closing the trade early to minimize losses.

7. Trading False Breakouts:

False breakouts occur when the price breaks through a support or resistance level but then quickly reverses, often trapping traders who entered the trade in the direction of the breakout. To avoid false breakouts, traders should wait for confirmation of the breakout before entering the trade and use other technical indicators to confirm the strength of the breakout.

In summary, trading breakouts involves identifying key levels of support or resistance, waiting for confirmation of the breakout, entering the trade in the direction of the breakout, setting stop-loss orders to manage risk, taking profits when the price reaches the target level, and monitoring the trade regularly. By following these steps and avoiding false breakouts, traders can maximize their profits and minimize their losses when trading breakouts in financial markets.

Chapter 5:

Using Trendlines for Entry and Exit Points

Trendlines are not only useful for identifying the direction of the trend and key levels of support and resistance, but they can also be used to determine entry and exit points for trades. Here are some strategies for using trendlines to determine entry and exit points:

1. Trendline Breakout Strategy:

One way to use trendlines for entry and exit points is to look for a breakout of the trendline. When the price breaks above a trendline in an uptrend, traders can enter a long position, and when the price breaks below a trendline in a downtrend, traders can enter a short position. Stop-loss orders can be placed below the breakout point to limit potential losses.

Trading a trendline Strategy:

a) Identify the Trendline:

The first step is to identify the trendline that is relevant to the current trend. An uptrend is characterized by a series of higher highs and higher lows, while a downtrend is characterized by a series of lower highs and lower lows. Draw a trendline connecting the higher lows in an uptrend or the lower highs in a downtrend.

b) Wait for the Breakout:

Once the trendline is identified, the trader must wait for the price to break above or below the trendline. In an uptrend, the breakout occurs when the price breaks above the trendline, and in a downtrend, the breakout occurs when the price breaks below the trendline.

c) Confirm the Breakout:

It's essential to confirm the breakout to ensure that it's a genuine breakout and not a false one. Look for confirmation in the form of volume or other technical indicators. If the volume is high when the price breaks through the trendline, it's a strong confirmation of the breakout.

d) Enter the Trade:

Once the breakout is confirmed, the trader can enter the trade. In an uptrend, the trader can enter a long position, and in a downtrend, the trader can enter a short position. The entry point should be slightly above the trendline in an uptrend and slightly below the trendline in a downtrend.

e) Place Stop-Loss Orders:

As with any trading strategy, risk management is crucial. The trader should place a stop-loss order below the breakout point in an uptrend and above the breakout point in a downtrend. The stop-loss order will limit the potential loss if the trade doesn't work out as planned.

f) Set Profit Targets:

Once the trade is entered, the trader should set profit targets based on their risk-reward ratio. A common practice is to set a profit target that's twice the size of the stop-loss order. For example, if the stop-loss order is set at 20 pips, the profit target should be set at 40 pips.

g) Monitor the Trade:

It's important to monitor the trade and adjust the stop-loss and profit targets as necessary. If the trade is going in the trader's favor, they may want to move the stop-loss order to lock in profits. If the trade is not going as planned, the trader may want to exit the trade and cut their losses.

In conclusion, a trendline breakout strategy can be an effective way to enter trades in the direction of the trend. By following these steps and implementing proper risk management techniques, traders can improve their chances of success when using this strategy.

Figure 7Trendline breakout strategy

2. Trendline Bounce Strategy:

Another way to use trendlines for entry and exit points is to look for a bounce off the trendline. In an uptrend, traders can enter a long position when the price bounces off the trendline and resumes its upward movement. In a downtrend, traders can enter a short position when the price bounces off the trendline and resumes its downward movement. Stop-loss orders can be placed below the trendline to limit potential losses.

Trading a trendline bounce strategy:

Here are the steps to trade a trendline bounce strategy:

a) Identify the Trendline:

The first step is to identify the trendline that is relevant to the current trend. An uptrend is characterized by a series of higher highs and higher lows, while a downtrend is characterized by a series of lower highs and lower lows. Draw a trendline connecting the higher lows in an uptrend or the lower highs in a downtrend.

b) Wait for the Price to Reach the Trendline:

Once the trendline is identified, the trader must wait for the price to reach the trendline. In an uptrend, the price will approach the trendline from below, while in a downtrend, the price will approach the trendline from above.

c) Look for Confirmation:

Once the price reaches the trendline, look for confirmation in the form of price action or other technical indicators. The trader should look for bullish price action if trading an uptrend and bearish price action if trading a downtrend. If the price action confirms a bounce off the trendline, the trader can proceed to the next step.

d) Enter the Trade:

Once the bounce is confirmed, the trader can enter the trade. In an uptrend, the trader can enter a long position, and in a downtrend, the trader can enter a short position. The entry point should be slightly above the trendline in an uptrend and slightly below the trendline in a downtrend.

e) Place Stop-Loss Orders:

As with any trading strategy, risk management is crucial. The trader should place a stop-loss order below the trendline in an uptrend and above the trendline in a downtrend. The stop-loss order will limit the potential loss if the trade doesn't work out as planned.

f) Set Profit Targets:

Once the trade is entered, the trader should set profit targets based on their risk-reward ratio. A common practice is to set a profit target that's twice the size of the stop-loss order. For example, if the stop-loss order is set at 20 pips, the profit target should be set at 40 pips.

g) Monitor the Trade:

It's important to monitor the trade and adjust the stop-loss and profit targets as necessary. If the trade is going in the trader's favor, they may want to move the stop-loss order to lock in profits. If the trade is not going as planned, the trader may want to exit the trade and cut their losses.

In conclusion, a trendline bounce strategy can be an effective way to enter trades in the direction of the trend. By following these steps and implementing proper risk management techniques, traders can improve their chances of success when using this strategy.

3. Trendline Retracement Strategy:

A third way to use trendlines for entry and exit points is to look for a retracement to the trendline. When the price retraces to a trendline in an uptrend, traders can enter a long position, and when the price retraces to a trendline in a downtrend, traders can enter a short position. Stop-loss orders can be placed below the trendline to limit potential losses.

Trading a Retracement Strategy:

Here are the steps to trade a trendline retracement strategy:

a) Identify the Trendline:

The first step is to identify the trendline that is relevant to the current trend. An uptrend is characterized by a series of higher highs and higher lows, while a downtrend is characterized by a series of lower highs and lower lows. Draw a trendline connecting the higher lows in an uptrend or the lower highs in a downtrend.

b) Wait for the Price to Retrace to the Trendline:

Once the trendline is identified, the trader must wait for the price to retrace to the trendline. In an uptrend, the price will retrace from a high and approach the trendline from above, while in a downtrend, the price will retrace from a low and approach the trendline from below.

c) Look for Confirmation:

Once the price retraces to the trendline, look for confirmation in the form of price action or other technical indicators. The trader should look for bullish price action if trading an uptrend and bearish price action if trading a downtrend. If the price action confirms a bounce off the trendline, the trader can proceed to the next step.

d) Enter the Trade:

Once the retracement is confirmed, the trader can enter the trade. In an uptrend, the trader can enter a long position, and in a downtrend, the trader can enter a short position. The entry point should be slightly above the retracement in an uptrend and slightly below the retracement in a downtrend.

e) Place Stop-Loss Orders:

As with any trading strategy, risk management is crucial. The trader should place a stop-loss order below the retracement in an uptrend and above the retracement in a downtrend. The stop-loss order will limit the potential loss if the trade doesn't work out as planned.

f) Set Profit Targets:

Once the trade is entered, the trader should set profit targets based on their risk-reward ratio. A common practice is to set a profit target that's twice the size of the stop-loss order. For example, if the stop-loss order is set at 20 pips, the profit target should be set at 40 pips.

g) Monitor the Trade:

It's important to monitor the trade and adjust the stop-loss and profit targets as necessary. If the trade is going in the trader's favor, they may want to move the stop-loss order to lock in profits. If the trade is not going as planned, the trader may want to exit the trade and cut their losses.

In conclusion, a trendline retracement strategy can be an effective way to enter trades in the direction of the trend. By following these steps and implementing proper risk management techniques, traders can improve their chances of success when using this strategy.

4. Trendline Channel Strategy:

A fourth way to use trendlines for entry and exit points is to use trendline channels. Trendline channels are created by drawing two parallel trendlines that contain the price movement within a channel. Traders can enter long positions when the price bounces off the lower trendline and enters the channel and enter short positions when the price bounces off the upper trendline and enters the channel. Stop-loss orders can be placed below the lower trendline for long positions and above the upper trendline for short positions.

Figure 8 Trendline Channel Strategy

Trading a Trendline Channel Strategy

Here are the steps to trade a trendline channel strategy:

a) Identify the Trendline Channel:

The first step is to identify the trendline channel that is relevant to the current trend. Draw a trendline connecting the higher highs and another trendline connecting the higher lows in an uptrend or the lower highs and lower lows in a downtrend.

b) Determine the Channel Range:

Once the trendline channel is identified, determine the range of the channel by looking at the distance between the trendlines. This range can be used to identify potential entry and exit points.

c) Look for Support and Resistance Levels:

Look for support and resistance levels within the channel. These levels can be identified by looking for areas where the price has bounced off the trendlines or where the price has stalled at a specific level.

d) Enter the Trade:

Once a support or resistance level is identified, the trader can enter a trade in the direction of the trend. In an uptrend, the trader can enter a long position when the price bounces off the lower trendline and approaches the upper trendline. In a downtrend, the trader can enter a short position when the price bounces off the upper trendline and approaches the lower trendline.

e) Place Stop-Loss Orders:

As with any trading strategy, risk management is crucial. The trader should place a stop-loss order below the lower trendline in an uptrend and above the upper trendline in a downtrend. The stop-loss order will limit the potential loss if the trade doesn't work out as planned.

f) Set Profit Targets:

Once the trade is entered, the trader should set profit targets based on their risk-reward ratio. A common practice is to set a profit target that's twice the size of the stop-loss order.

g) Monitor the Trade:

It's important to monitor the trade and adjust the stop-loss and profit targets as necessary. If the trade is going in the trader's favor, they may want to move the stop-loss order to lock in profits. If the trade is not going as planned, the trader may want to exit the trade and cut their losses.

In conclusion, a trendline channel strategy can be an effective way to enter trades in the direction of the trend while minimizing risk. By following these steps and implementing proper risk management techniques, traders can improve their chances of success when using this strategy.

5. Trendline Confluence Strategy:

A fifth way to use trendlines for entry and exit points is to look for confluence with other technical indicators. When trendlines intersect with other technical indicators such as moving averages, Fibonacci levels, or other trendlines, traders can use these areas of confluence as entry and exit points. Stop-loss orders can be placed below the trendline or other technical indicator to limit potential losses.

Trading a Tendline Confluence Strategy

Here are the steps to trade a trendline confluence strategy:

a) Identify the Trendlines:

The first step is to identify the trendlines that are relevant to the current trend. Draw a trendline connecting the higher highs and another trendline connecting the higher lows in an uptrend or the lower highs and lower lows in a downtrend.

b) Look for Confluence:

Look for areas where multiple trendlines intersect or converge. These areas will create a strong support or resistance level.

c) Determine Entry and Exit Points:

Once a trendline confluence area is identified, the trader can determine potential entry and exit points. In an uptrend, the trader can enter a long position when the price bounces off the confluence area and approaches the upper trendline. In a downtrend, the trader can enter a short position when the price bounces off the confluence area and approaches the lower trendline.

d) Place Stop-Loss Orders:

As with any trading strategy, risk management is crucial. The trader should place a stop-loss order below the confluence area in an uptrend and above the confluence area in a downtrend. The stop-loss order will limit the potential loss if the trade doesn't work out as planned.

e) Set Profit Targets:

Once the trade is entered, the trader should set profit targets based on their risk-reward ratio. A common practice is to set a profit target that's twice the size of the stop-loss order.

f) Monitor the Trade:

It's important to monitor the trade and adjust the stop-loss and profit targets as necessary. If the trade is going in the trader's favor, they may want to move the stop-loss order to lock in profits. If the trade is not going as planned, the trader may want to exit the trade and cut their losses.

In conclusion, a trendline confluence strategy can be an effective way to identify strong support and resistance levels and enter trades in the direction of the trend. By following these steps and implementing proper risk management techniques, traders can improve their chances of success when using this strategy.

In summary, trendlines can be used to determine entry and exit points for trades using various strategies such as the trendline breakout strategy, trendline bounce strategy, trendline retracement strategy, trendline channel strategy, and trendline confluence strategy.

By using trendlines in combination with other technical indicators, traders can improve their accuracy and profitability when entering and exiting trades in financial markets.

Chapter 6:

Risk Management

Effective risk management is one of the most important aspects of forex trading. No matter how skilled a trader is, there is always a risk of losing money in the market. Therefore, traders need to have a solid risk management plan in place to protect their capital and minimize potential losses.

Here are some key strategies for managing risk in forex trading:

1. Set Stop-Loss Orders

Stop-loss orders are an essential risk management tool for forex traders. A stop-loss order is an order to sell a security when it reaches a certain price level, limiting the trader's potential losses. It's important to set stop-loss orders at the appropriate level to avoid losing more than what's acceptable.

Traders should use technical analysis to identify key levels of support and resistance, and then set their stop-loss orders accordingly. For example, if a trader buys a currency pair at 1.2000 and sets a stop-loss order at 1.1950, they are limiting their potential losses to 50 pips.

2. Use Proper Position Sizing

Proper position sizing ensures that traders are not risking more than they can afford to lose on any given trade. The general rule of thumb is to risk no more than 1-2% of the trading account balance on any one trade.

For example, if a trader has a trading account with a balance of $10,000, they should not risk more than $100-$200 on any one trade. Proper position sizing helps to minimize potential losses and preserve capital over the long term.

3. Diversify Your Trades

Diversification is an important risk management strategy for forex traders. By diversifying their trades, traders can spread out their risk and avoid over-exposure to any single currency pair.

For example, a trader may choose to trade multiple currency pairs rather than focusing on just one. This helps to spread out the risk and reduce the impact of any single trade on the overall trading account.

Use Leverage Wisely

Leverage is a powerful tool that can amplify potential gains in forex trading. However, it can also amplify potential losses. It's important to use leverage wisely and avoid over-leveraging.

Traders should understand the risks associated with leverage and use it conservatively. A general rule of thumb is to use no more than 10:1 leverage, which means that for every $1 in the trading account, the trader can trade up to $10 in the market.

4. Stay Up-to-Date on Market News

Unexpected news events can cause significant market volatility and increase risk. By staying up-to-date on market news, traders can adjust their trading strategy accordingly.

Traders should follow economic news releases and be aware of any significant political or geopolitical events that could impact the markets. By keeping a close eye on market news, traders can make informed decisions and adjust their risk management strategies as needed.

5. Maintain Emotional Control

Emotional control is critical to effective risk management. It's important to avoid making impulsive decisions based on fear or greed. Traders should remain disciplined and stick to their trading plan, even during times of market volatility.

Traders can practice emotional control by setting realistic trading goals, maintaining a positive mindset, and avoiding over-trading. By maintaining emotional control, traders can make rational decisions and minimize potential losses in the market.

In conclusion, effective risk management is crucial to success in forex trading. By implementing these risk management strategies, traders can minimize potential losses and increase their chances of success in the market.

Chapter 7:

Backtesting and Optimization

Backtesting and optimization are essential processes in forex trading, helping traders evaluate the effectiveness of their trading strategies and identify areas for improvement. Backtesting involves testing a trading strategy using historical data to determine its potential profitability. Optimization involves refining the trading strategy to improve its performance based on backtesting results. Here are some key steps to follow when backtesting and optimizing a trading strategy:

1. Define Trading Strategy Rules

Before backtesting a trading strategy, traders should define the rules for entry and exit points, stop-loss orders, and take-profit orders. The rules should be clear and well-defined to ensure consistency when backtesting and optimizing.

2. Gather Historical Data

Traders should gather historical data for the currency pairs they plan to trade. The data should include price and volume information for a specific time frame, such as daily or hourly data.

3. Backtest the Trading Strategy

Using backtesting software, traders can test their trading strategy using historical data. Backtesting results can help traders evaluate the effectiveness of their trading strategy and identify areas for improvement.

4. Optimize the Trading Strategy

Based on backtesting results, traders can refine their trading strategy to improve its performance. Optimization involves adjusting the trading strategy rules, such as the stop-loss or take-profit levels, to maximize profitability while minimizing risk.

5. Evaluate the Results

After optimizing the trading strategy, traders should evaluate the results to determine its effectiveness. The results should be compared to the original backtesting results to determine whether the optimization process improved the trading strategy's performance.

6. Implement the Trading Strategy

Once traders have backtested and optimized their trading strategy, they can implement it in live trading. Traders should continue to monitor the strategy's performance and make adjustments as needed.

In conclusion, backtesting and optimization are essential processes in forex trading, helping traders evaluate the effectiveness of their trading strategies and identify areas for improvement. By defining trading strategy rules, gathering historical data, backtesting the trading strategy, optimizing the trading strategy, evaluating the results, and implementing the trading strategy, traders can improve their trading performance and increase their profitability.

Chapter 8:

Trading Psychology and Emotional Control

Trading psychology is a critical aspect of forex trading. It refers to the mindset and emotions that traders experience while trading, and how they can impact their trading decisions and performance. Here are some key elements of trading psychology and emotional control that traders should consider:

a) Control Your Emotions

Emotions such as fear, greed, and anxiety are common among traders and can lead to poor decision-making. Fear can cause traders to hesitate and miss out on profitable trades, while greed can lead to overtrading and taking unnecessary risks. Anxiety can also be a hindrance to trading performance, causing traders to second-guess their decisions or make impulsive trades.

To control emotions, traders should be aware of their emotions and their impact on trading decisions. They should take breaks when feeling overwhelmed or stressed, and practice relaxation techniques such as deep breathing or meditation. Traders can also use positive self-talk and visualization to boost confidence and reduce anxiety.

b) Set Realistic Expectations

Forex trading is not a get-rich-quick scheme, and traders should set realistic expectations for their trading performance. This means avoiding unrealistic goals and focusing on making consistent profits over the long term. Traders should also avoid comparing themselves to other traders or benchmarks, as this can create unnecessary pressure and lead to poor decision-making.

Setting realistic goals and expectations requires traders to do their research and have a solid understanding of the market and their trading strategy. It's also important to be patient and recognize that trading success takes time and effort.

c) Manage Risk

Effective risk management is crucial for forex trading success. Traders should use proper position sizing and set stop-loss orders to limit their risk exposure. This means only risking a small percentage of their trading account on each trade and avoiding overleveraging.

Traders should also have a plan for managing losses, such as adjusting stop-loss orders or closing out losing trades early. By managing risk effectively, traders can protect their trading capital and avoid significant losses.

d) Stick to Your Trading Plan

Traders should have a well-defined trading plan that outlines their entry and exit points, risk management strategies, and overall trading goals. It's important to stick to this plan and avoid deviating from it based on emotions or market news.

To stick to a trading plan, traders should stay disciplined and avoid impulsive trades. They should also review their trading plan regularly and make adjustments as needed based on market conditions or performance data.

e) Monitor Your Mental State

Trading can be a stressful and emotionally taxing activity, and it's important to take care of mental health and well-being. Traders should be aware of their mental state while trading and take breaks as needed to avoid burnout or emotional exhaustion.

To monitor mental state, traders can use self-assessment tools or keep a trading journal to track their emotions and performance. They can also seek support from a mentor or trading community to discuss challenges and get feedback.

f) Learn from Mistakes

Mistakes are a natural part of the learning process, and traders should view them as opportunities for growth and improvement. By analyzing past trading mistakes, traders can identify areas for improvement and refine their trading strategy.

To learn from mistakes, traders should keep a trading journal and review it regularly. They should also seek feedback from other traders or a mentor and use this feedback to make adjustments to their trading strategy.

g) Stay Disciplined

Discipline is critical for trading success. Traders should follow their trading plan, manage risk effectively, and avoid impulsive trades based on emotions. This requires mental toughness and a strong commitment to trading goals and objectives.

To stay disciplined, traders should focus on the process rather than the outcome. They should also use positive reinforcement and reward themselves for sticking to their trading plan or achieving their trading goals.

In conclusion, trading psychology and emotional control are critical aspects of forex trading. By controlling emotions, setting realistic expectations, managing risk, sticking to a trading plan, monitoring mental state, learning from mistakes

Chapter 9:

Monitoring and Adjusting

Trading in the forex market is not a one-time event; it requires ongoing monitoring and adjustment. Monitoring refers to keeping an eye on the trades that you have opened and assessing their progress. Adjusting refers to making changes to your trading plan or strategy based on the observations and insights gathered during the monitoring process.

In this chapter, we will discuss the importance of monitoring your trades, how to go about it, and how to adjust your trading strategy to improve your performance.

Importance of Monitoring

Monitoring your trades is essential because it enables you to identify any potential problems early on, before they escalate into major issues. By monitoring your trades, you can quickly detect any trends, patterns, or anomalies that could affect your trades' outcome. Moreover, monitoring your trades helps you stay informed about the overall market conditions and make better-informed trading decisions.

How to Monitor Your Trades

Monitoring your trades involves tracking several parameters, including:

Entry and exit points: Keep track of the entry and exit points for each of your trades. This will help you identify which trades are performing well and which ones are not.

a) Risk management:

Keep an eye on your risk management parameters, such as stop-loss levels, position sizing, and risk-reward ratios. This will help you ensure that you are not taking on too much risk.

b) Market conditions:

Monitor the market conditions regularly to stay informed about any changes that could affect your trades. This includes tracking economic indicators, news releases, and geopolitical events.

c) Performance metrics:

Track your trading performance metrics, such as win/loss ratio, average gain/loss, and maximum drawdown. This will help you assess your overall performance and identify areas that need improvement.

d) How to Adjust Your Trading Strategy

Adjusting your trading strategy involves making changes to your plan based on the observations made during the monitoring process. Here are some tips on how to adjust your trading strategy:

Analyze your trades: Analyze the trades that are not performing well and identify the reasons for their poor performance. This could be due to incorrect analysis, poor timing, or inadequate risk management.

e) Identify patterns:

Look for patterns in your trading performance and adjust your strategy accordingly. For example, if you notice that you tend to enter trades too early or too late, adjust your entry and exit criteria accordingly.

Modify your risk management: If you find that you are consistently losing money due to poor risk management, adjust your stop-loss levels, position sizing, or risk-reward ratio.

f) Stay disciplined:

It's essential to stick to your trading plan and avoid making impulsive decisions based on emotions or short-term market conditions.

Conclusion

Monitoring and adjusting your trades are essential aspects of forex trading. By keeping an eye on your trades and making adjustments to your trading plan, you can improve your trading performance and achieve better results over time. Remember to stay disciplined, and don't let emotions cloud your judgment.

Chapter 10:

Recovering from Losses in Forex Trading

Recovering from losses in forex trading can be a challenging and emotional process. However, there are several strategies you can implement to help minimize your losses and recover your account balance.

1. Cut Your Losses Early

One of the most effective ways to recover from losses is to cut them early. This means implementing stop-loss orders to limit your potential losses on a trade. By setting a stop-loss, you can exit a trade before it turns against you, thereby preventing a significant loss.

2. Trade Smaller Positions

If you've experienced significant losses, it may be wise to trade smaller positions until you've regained your confidence and rebuilt your account balance. Trading smaller positions will also help you minimize your risk and limit your potential losses.

3. Re-evaluate Your Trading Plan

It's essential to evaluate your trading plan when you experience losses. You may need to adjust your strategies, risk management rules, or trading approach to reduce your losses and improve your overall profitability.

4. Seek Professional Help

If you're struggling to recover from losses, consider seeking the help of a professional trader or a trading coach. They can help you identify weaknesses in your trading plan, offer advice on improving your trading strategies, and provide emotional support during challenging times.

5. Maintain Emotional Control

Finally, it's crucial to maintain emotional control while recovering from losses. Avoid making impulsive trading decisions or trying to chase after losses. Stay focused on your trading plan and be patient in your efforts to recover your account balance.

Remember, the forex market is unpredictable, and losses are an inevitable part of trading. By implementing these strategies and maintaining a disciplined approach to trading, you can minimize your losses and increase your chances of recovering your account balance.

Chapter 11:

When to Withdraw Your Profits

One of the most exciting aspects of forex trading is the potential to generate significant profits. However, deciding when to withdraw your profits can be a challenging decision that requires careful consideration. Here are some factors to consider when deciding when to withdraw your forex profits:

1. Set Realistic Profit Targets

Before you start trading, set realistic profit targets for each trade and overall. This will help you avoid being overly greedy and help you lock in profits as soon as they become available.

2. Maintain a Trading Plan

Maintaining a trading plan that includes profit targets and exit strategies can help you make more informed decisions about when to take profits. Stick to your plan, and avoid being swayed by emotional impulses or market fluctuations.

3. Monitor Market Conditions

Regularly monitoring market conditions can help you identify potential opportunities to take profits. Pay attention to news events, economic data releases, and technical analysis indicators to help you make more informed trading decisions.

4. Don't Overtrade

Overtrading can increase your risk and make it more challenging to take profits consistently. Stick to your trading plan, limit your position sizes, and avoid chasing the markets.

5. Take Profits Incrementally

Taking profits incrementally can help you minimize your risk and lock in profits as soon as they become available. Consider scaling out of your trades by taking partial profits at predetermined intervals.

6. Reinvest Profits

Reinvesting your profits can help you grow your account balance over time. Consider using some of your profits to fund new trades or diversify your portfolio to minimize your risk exposure.

7. Consider Your Personal Financial Situation

Consider your personal financial situation when deciding when to withdraw your profits. If you need the money for immediate expenses or have other financial obligations, consider withdrawing some or all of your profits to meet these obligations.

In conclusion, deciding when to withdraw your profits requires a disciplined approach and a consideration of various factors. By setting realistic profit targets, maintaining a trading plan, monitoring market conditions, avoiding overtrading, taking profits incrementally, reinvesting profits, and considering your personal financial situation, you can make more informed decisions about when to take profits and grow your forex trading account over time.

Final word

Forex trading can be an exciting and rewarding endeavor, but it also requires discipline, patience, and a willingness to learn. By using trendlines as part of your trading strategy, you can gain a better understanding of market trends and potential trading opportunities.

When using trendlines, it's essential to remember that they are just one tool in your trading arsenal. It's important to consider other factors such as support and resistance levels, market conditions, and risk management when making trading decisions.

In addition, it's crucial to maintain emotional control and avoid impulsive trading decisions that can lead to significant losses. By adhering to a trading plan, setting realistic profit targets, and monitoring market conditions, you can make more informed trading decisions and increase your chances of success.

Finally, always remember to keep learning and adapting your trading strategies to changing market conditions. Regularly reviewing and analyzing your trades, backtesting your strategies, and seeking out educational resources can help you improve your skills and become a more successful forex trader.

With discipline, perseverance, and a commitment to continuous learning, you can build a profitable trading career using trendlines and other tools at your disposal.